18 Wheels of Justice

Are you and your Staff Prepared?

Real World Trucking Negotiating Strategy designed for beginners and seasoned veterans alike. For Owner Operators, Small Fleets and Carriers.

www.18WheelsofJustice.com

18wheelsofjusticethebook.blogspot.com

ISBN 10 1477682481

ISBN 13 9781477682487

"THE BOOK"

Negotiating with Freight Brokers & 3PL's

18 Wheels of Justice

Michael H. Komadina

www.18wheelsofjustice.com

PREFACE

This book is dedicated to God, my son, Joseph, the love of my life, Kitalena, without the support of all of them; this book wouldn't have been possible. It is also dedicated to my parents, Tom and Donna Komadina, who were pioneers and visionaries in the Freight Brokerage business in the mid 1980's, when de-regulation opened the Industry for the Freight Broker. Donna, my Mom, who was a driving force in my life and taught me the brokerage business, passed away in 2007. God Bless her. I spent my summer breaks while in high school trying to book loads with carriers, often between my times spent on the forklift loading trucks. There were many times I had to explain to carriers what exactly a "broker" was. I later switched to the trucking side of the business and

realized the trucking business was by far my favorite. My Dad taught me the trucking business, and we would have long, sometimes, heated debates at night about ideas and the best approach to trucking. I have owned and operated many trucking and brokerage companies over the years. I hope this book will help you be more successful and truly get what you deserve for the risk and hard work involved in our business.

Thank you for buying this book!

Mike Komadina

www.18WheelsofJustice.com

CONTENTS

SECTION I – PROVEN BUSINESS PRACTICES

SECTION II – #1 RULE OF NEGOTIATING

SECTION III – BASIC STAGES OF NEGOTIATION

SECTION IV – STRATEGIES! - PUTTING INTO PRACTICE MEANS ADDITIONAL PROFITS. EVERY SINGLE LOAD NEGOTIATON SHOULD INCLUDE AT LEAST 10 OF THESE STRATEGIES, TRY TO USE THEM ALL!

SECTION I – PROVEN BUSINESS PRACTICES

1) BROKERS AND 3PL's AS CUSTOMERS

The business of shipping products to customers is ever-evolving into a world in which 3PL's and Freight Brokers are able to control more and more of the truckload market. Large manufacturer's want to focus more on their core business, than having entire shipping departments dedicated to rates and setting up carriers, dealing with scheduling appointments and so on.

So, what does this mean to you? A brave soul, the lone owner operator who sets out to seek his fortune with his own truck and trailer? A small carrier with a dozen or so trucks, trying to build a dynasty or family fortune?

A medium to large carrier whose business is 30% to 40% broker & 3PL freight and have a planner or dispatcher unprepared or untrained in the art of negotiation? Yes, and it is an art, when done creatively, properly and successfully, negotiating can be one of the most beautiful and rewarding experiences one can have.

Think back to the days of your youth, negotiating with parents to stay up later, only to be told to go to bed. Or did you return to the negotiating table with your parents armed with opposing arguments? How about delicately trying to negotiate your first kiss with a blushing, young redhead and getting a hug or handshake? Or did you steal a kiss and walk away, leaving her wanting more?

Like most of us, you probably have memories of good and bad negotiations. The important

NOTES -

thing to remember is that you walked away from each negotiation with more knowledge, experience and skill.

NOTES –

The transportation business has changed over the last ten years. What does it mean to you?

OPPORTUNITY

MORE PROFIT

AND MORE PROFIT

CONTOL OF YOUR BUSINESS

CONTROL OF YOUR DESTINY

There are tens of thousands of creditworthy brokers and 3PL's today. The opportunities are endless and better than ever from the carrier and owner operator perspective.

Why? Because you don't have to spend six months to a year making sales calls on the local furniture manufacturer or beer distributor to get your first truckload of profitable freight. Typically, you can't

NOTES -

service, or for that matter, don't want all of their freight anyway.

Some of our best and often overlooked customers are the 3PL's and freight brokers. No longer are they just a backhaul provider or someone who we call last, they can be some of our best customers!

NOTES -

2) HONESTY

Mom was right, honesty is the best policy. It is the best way to live and conduct business. There are many times when it is easier to tell a broker that the truck broke down, or some other story, but the reality is that the truth is always the best way to go. This is true for letting them know what time your truck will be empty, whether or not you are able to deliver on time, or your truck or trucks are overbooked. If, at anytime you have to give a load back, do it right away and be honest about it. Don't wait until the last minute to give the load back. Not only is it the right thing to do, but it you will come out much better off in the long run. Don't ever book a load as a back up and hope something better comes along. This is a losing strategy. Negotiate a rate that works for you or don't take the load. Once you have committed to the load forget about the price and do the

NOTES -

best job you can. Treat every load you haul as if it is for your best customer. This will pay off for many years to come as you build and maintain your reputation as a world class carrier.

NOTES –

3) COMMITMENT

Once you commit to a load, regardless of price, it is your load. It doesn't matter if your best customer calls you after you hang up the phone with a Broker/3PL, with a better load, stay on the load you have committed to. This is a long term strategy to success. Your word is your bond with a Broker/3PL. Many times they aren't committed to a load until they have a truck for the load, so, if you give the load back to them, they have to give the load back to their customer. This will strain and may destroy any previous "good will" created in your relationship. Now, if the parameters of the load changes for any reason, delivery appointment, weight, and extra stop, etc. This should be viewed as an extra profit opportunity and should be leveraged to your advantage. If they are unwilling to pay for

NOTES -

this additional cost you are incurring, feel free to give the load back to the Broker/3PL.

4) INTEGRITY

This is a basic tenet of good business and is heard time and time again for a reason. There is no better feeling of hearing from a Broker/3PL that you have hauled loads for in the past, and have a relationship with. They see your truck posted and call you first. They remember you or they look at notes on your company from previous loads. This builds the confidence needed to pay you a higher than usual price for hauling their load. The additional money they will pay you for this load because of your integrity and history with them is nothing compared to the piece of mind and good service they provide their customer. This will result in additional business for years to come for the Broker/3PL and for you.

NOTES -

5) PRIDE

Take pride in what you do! Transporting goods and products across this great nation of ours is instrumental to the well being of all Americans. Take pride in your name and reputation. Treat every Broker/3PL with respect regardless of size, possibility of doing business again, etc.

Never burn a bridge with a Broker/3PL, always do whatever you can to right a wrong you may have caused with them. If they can't overcome an honest mistake, talk to their supervisor, if that fails, then move on.

NOTES -

SECTION II - #1 RULE OF NEGOTIATION

NOTES -

1) Ability to stay calm, likeable, affable, specific and subtle during all stages of negotiation. Try and remember C.L.A.S.S.

C – Calm

L – Likeable

A – Affable (polite)

S – Specific (don't generalize)

S – Subtle (don't be demanding)

This is not a stage or form of negotiation, but this is a must! If this is not achieved and maintained, the odds drop significantly of a successful negotiation for this load!!

I will repeat this often through out this book, because this approach must be brought with you to the negotiating table every time.

What does C.L.A.S.S. mean? It doesn't mean tell jokes, ask them about their week-end plans, etc. It simply means stick to the

NOTES -

business at hand. Be appreciative of the fact that they are offering you business. Every load is not a "good fit" for you, don't take it personally nor give your opinion of the load they are offering you. It may be a customer that they worked hard to get, and other carriers may have taken the load cheaper previously for a variety of reasons. If it doesn't work for you, it doesn't work. Don't get emotional or frustrated while booking loads.

Negotiations are a game, try to enjoy them. Compliment the other person in a sincere way, when possible. Compliment the company, your long standing relationship or how you always get good loads from them. Compliment them about how "their money is good", you never have to worry about getting paid. Tell them how you always wanted to, or enjoy taking loads from them, you have heard about them and how good they are to work with.

NOTES -

If they take the time to set you up with them as a new carrier, thank them for doing that!

There are many ways to create good will, practice this approach.

Every conversation you have with a broker/3PL should create good will between you, whether you take the load or not. Practice, Practice, Practice...

NOTES -

NOTES -

NOTES -

SECTION III

THE BASIC STAGES OF NEGOTIATION

NOTES -

1) PRE-NEGOTIATION OR "FRAMING" – "SETTING THE STAGE"

This may seem like simple and basic knowledge, but we must dissect the stages of negotiation to truly understand the process.

BROKER/3PL Calls about the truck you have posted in Chicago. He asks you a variety of questions, what's your MC? Are we "set up"? Is your truck empty now? Can he load by 3pm? Can he scale 44,000? Is it an air ride trailer? Can he deliver at 7am tomorrow in St. Louis?

The Broker/3PL is an interested buyer of your services, the more of these criteria you meet, the higher the value of your service for this single transaction. Be patient here and answer slowly, checking to make sure

NOTES -

you meet these criteria, thus, increasing the value of your service. Throw in self serving comments such as, "he is one of our better drivers", "I just hung up with the driver a few minutes ago, he is waiting, ready to go,", "this load just might work for us, let's discuss"...etc. "Yes, we are set up with you; let me check your credit history to make sure we are ok to take this load". Put them on hold for 30 seconds and come back and tell them, "Yes, you guys are good to go, you're a good broker, let's discuss this load some more". This creates mutual good will subtly in your negotiation. This may be a 60 second conversation so far, but drag it out longer while you look up the broker, their history, their credibility. The more time the Broker/3PL has in the transaction, the more he has invested it in and wants to see it work.

NOTES –

It's not about establishing a rate at this point. You are framing, you are bringing up the value of your services for this particular transaction at this moment in time. You are framing his opinion, by convincing him quietly of how low his chances of finding a more suitable "partner" for this load. And by quietly, I mean patiently waiting and letting him figure it out for himself. If he can't or doesn't realize it after a minute or two, then tell him! Now, or later in the negotiation. This can be an excellent "back burner" item, when getting final price later.

Now you have established that you meet the Broker/3PL and your own criteria for a successful transaction, and when everybody is friendly and quietly anticipating a "deal" the fun begins....

NOTES -

2) DEADLOCK, STALEMATE AND ARRESTED DEVELOPMENT

This is a beautiful time in the load booking process. The longer the Broker/3PL is on the phone, the better your chances of getting the rate you deserve.

Here is where the true negotiating begins. Remember the "heart" of the sale or negotiation doesn't truly start until someone says "NO".

One, two or any combination of the following 15 negotiating strategies and tactics can be employed during the deadlock. The key is to be patient; you are in no hurry to take this load, as your services are valuable and in demand! Pausing to take another call will make him assume you are talking to another Broker/3PL. You can mention that it is another Broker/3PL on the phone, but give your Broker/3PL your full attention!

NOTES -

Don't make him feel that you are currently negotiating with another Broker/3PL while you are on the phone with him. This is rude, and will not end well. Let him know that he has the full potential to utilize this valuable asset you have offered him, while you are still in active negotiations. It is not a good idea to attempt to coerce someone into paying you the price you need, by offering services simultaneously to another "suitor" and using that as a bargaining chip. It will do nothing but insult the Broker/3PL and cheapen your relationship. We want to remain gentlemen throughout this process and behave as such.

You can casually suggest that other Brokers/3PL's are calling about the same truck, but assure him that, the opportunity to use your truck is available to him only while you are negotiating. We want to create goodwill here. He will be going to his boss or

NOTES -

customer to get approval for the higher rate he is going to pay you, and he doesn't want to do that and take a chance that your truck will not be available when he comes back to you with a much higher rate.

Always have this book at the ready while you are on the phone, it will come naturally to you after some time, but it will take practice to develop your own style. New ideas and approaches will come from using this book over time, using a technique in a situation you didn't see before.

NOTES -

3) ACCEPTANCE AND SETTLEMENT OF NEGOTIATION. A TRANSACTION IS BORN!

You have just negotiated a good load! It may be the best load you have ever gotten out of a certain area and you feel flush with victory.

Do not gloat, but remain humble and likeable.

You never want the Broker/3PL to feel taken advantage of; he needs to feel good about the transaction and he should! Every argument you presented is valid and real. You want him walking away feeling as good as you do about the load.

Get it in writing! Always have them email the rate confirmation to you while you are on the phone with them whenever possible. Emails take a few seconds and once you have it, there can be no disagreements. 90% of

NOTES -

Broker/3PL companies are very ethical, but there are always a few pretenders.

Another carrier who hasn't been blessed with the wisdom of buying this book may call 30 seconds after you hang up and take the load for half the price you agreed to take it for. We don't want to lose our hard fought rate and load over not following up on details at the end. Don't push too hard, but I always want to see it in front of me before I hang up. I let them know, politely, that I would like to wait on the phone to make sure I have it. "Email is better so someone else doesn't grab it off the fax and we need to be sure I have all the information we need to make sure this load is picked up and delivered without any issues." After all this is the most important load you are doing and this is another way to reinforce this with the Broker/3PL.

NOTES -

SECTION IV –

STRATEGIES!! PUTTING INTO PRACTICE MEANS ADDITIONAL PROFITS.

EVERY SINGLE LOAD NEGOTIATON SHOULD INCLUDE AT LEAST 10 OF THESE STRATEGIES – TRY TO USE THEM ALL EVERYTIME!!

NOTES -

STRATEGY 1 – POSTING TRUCKS

Never call a Broker/3PL about a posted load if at all possible. Always post your truck and let them call you. This gives you a lot of bargaining power from the start. They are calling you trying to "sell" you a load. This isn't a load you need nor necessarily want, let them sell it to you. Unless you need to go to a certain area, always post the destination as open. This will bring up a lot of interesting opportunities.

Repost your truck every hour or so, this let's the Broker/3PL know it is actively available. Think of fishing, and using fresh bait.

NOTES -

STRATEGY 2 – NEVER BRING UP PRICE; ALWAYS HAVE BROKER/3PL GIVE PRICE FIRST

Let the Broker/3PL bring up price! Never give a rate first. You don't know what the load pays! There are many times when you will be surprised that it is higher than you would have asked for. Let him throw his rate out there. Often, it will be in the context of "I usually move these for "X". If it is really low, then dismiss it as not for you and attempt to get off the phone.

Remain polite and likeable, comments such as," that's a garbage load, I don't haul cheap freight" are not appropriate. Remember C.L.A.S.S.

Remember he is calling you, if he states he usually moves it for that price then politely advise him to call some of his regular carriers.

NOTES -

More than likely he will ask you what you need. Again, never bring up a price. Be non-committal and ask him what he thinks the best rate is that he can do on the load.

When he gives you his "best rate" this should become your "anchor" or starting point for negotiating. Typically, with sophisticated Brokers/3PL's, his best rate is the maximum rate they want to pay while holding onto their minimum profit target for this particular load.

NOTES -

STRATEGY 3 – PATIENCE

Take your time. This is the only revenue your truck will generate for the next day or two or three. Every load is important and has additional profit in it. Let the Broker/3PL talk and you listen. Never interrupt!! Listen for clues as to how badly they want to move the load. Did another carrier fall off of it? Is it a new customer for them? Is it a new lane for an existing customer of theirs? Have they had problems with their customer and need a reliable carrier for the load? These are all issues that give you more negotiating power, the more you listen the more you will learn. Talking only serves to give away your power, unless you are complimenting the broker or discussing your strengths as a carrier.

NOTES -

STRATEGY 4 – KNOW THE REALISTIC RATE STARTING POINT

This is very important. If Broker/3PL thinks you are way off base with the rate you want to haul the load for, you lose your credibility.

If he is offering a good rate, by all means tell him so and agree. Compliment him on his ability to price loads correctly. But again, it is a good rate for someone else, not you in your current situation right here, right now. Then give him the reasons why... You have to build your arguments to get him to agree to your reasoning on why you need a better than "good" rate. "Framing"

NOTES -

STRATEGY 5 – HELLO THIRD PARTY!

Your negotiation is going fairly well; it has been friendly and easy going. You have assured him you can do this particular load successfully, will meet all of his needs and in the end it will be good for him and his customer. He needs reassurance at this point, that you are definitely interested in hauling this load; it will be good for all involved.

Now, ask him if he can hold for a minute while you double check to see if rate is ok with one of the following people:

BOSS

PARTNER

NOTES -

FRIEND

WIFE

EX-WIFE

DRIVER/OWNER OPERATOR WHO WILL BE HAULING LOAD, IF NOT YOURSELF

FATHER

SON

MOTHER

DAUGHTER

SPIRITUAL ADVISOR – Priest, Minister or Rabbi. Yes, the decision to take a load is this important.

NOTES -

Someone other than yourself who you need their approval to take the load or with whom you place value in their opinion and always run loads by them. If you don't have someone like this, you should find someone.

Feel free to introduce this third party at anytime during the load booking process. I find it most effective to introduce midway through the negotiation. It's your call, in the beginning or middle, but never at the end. If introduced early it can ease the tension with booking the load. By statements such as, "well, he isn't going to like that, that will be hard to convince him to take the load because it doesn't deliver until 2pm, may not be able to get reloaded in time the same day, etc" This creates a camaraderie between you and the Broker/3PL. Always remember you are trying to build a long term relationship.

NOTES -

This is a good thing. You and the Broker/3PL are teaming up together to convince this third party. Introducing the third party late in the negotiating can be seen as a cheap negotiating ploy and ruin all the goodwill you have created.

NOTES -

STRATEGY 6 – KNOW WHEN TO HOLD 'EM

Keep them on "ice"... Put them on hold while you are deciding what to do. Patience is a virtue. Patience, Patience, Patience. Are you already at a higher rate than you expected? How much more money will turn this from a good load into a great load? Another $200, $300 or more? Don't get too greedy, but, remember the additional money you get now is sweet, sweet, profit. Have your reasons prepared before you come back and tell them another $200 and let's do it. The longer they remain on hold the better. Don't let them stay on hold for longer than 60 seconds without picking up the phone and thanking them for their patience and reassuring them you want to do this load, and you are getting it worked out while they are on hold. The longer they are on hold, the more time and effort they have invested in selling this load to you, the more they want to wrap it up and move on to the next load.

NOTES -

STRATEGY 7 – KNOW WHEN TO MUTE 'EM

Did I say put them on hold? I meant put them on mute!! And listen. Like a deer hunter in the woods, waiting patiently, silently and listening for a twig to snap or a grunt in the distance.

It seems wrong, but it feels so right.

What are you listening for? Discussions between Broker/3PL with his co-workers on how bad they need to move this load, how they are about to lose this customer because of service problems?

Discussions on whether or not they have other options for this particular load. If you are their only option, then, more often than not, this means they are willing to take a loss on this load to save the customer. Maybe they discuss how they have to leave to go to

NOTES –

a doctor's appointment or want to go to lunch, etc. Listen for reasons they want to get this load moved and off of their plate. Sometimes they will discuss the highest they are willing to pay to get this load moved! Their loss is your gain. Why would they take a loss like that? Most successful broker/3PL's take a broad view of the entire account. They make money on most loads and take losses on other loads. All of this information helps you decide how much to increase your final rate to haul the load. Once you give your final rate, do not go back and ask for more, period. Remember your word in your negotiation is the key to your credibility and success!

NOTES -

STRATEGY 8 – HAVE COUNTERPOINTS PREPARED

Put together your own personal list of what makes a load attractive or unattractive to you, your driver, and your company. Have it with you at all times.

It can be personal reasons, too. I wanted to be home this week-end. My driver wanted to be home this week-end. I don't like the Northeast, Southeast, or length of haul, etc.

Have your own list prepared – There are note sections throughout this book for a reason! Please write in your own thoughts and ideas and always have them at the ready. There is always something you would have liked to bring up when you are on the phone and will remember as soon as you hang up! Have this information and this book at your fingertips. Take notes!!

NOTES -

STRATEGY 9 – TIMING IS EVERYTHING

If a Broker/3PL calls with a load that has an early loading time, 2pm and your truck is empty already at 9am. That adds a lot of value to your truck. If its 9am, that doesn't give him a lot of time to cover the load with someone else. Again put them on hold, while you decide how much more to ask for.

If it's 2pm and they want a truck at the shipper to load before 4pm and your truck can be there. Ask for the best amount they can do, and then describe the reasons that make the load unattractive to you. Let them know you are trying to make it work and ask them to hold. Come back with a premium rate. They will pay a premium for your truck. This is why patience and the hold button are so important, so you can review all the details of the situation and get the rate you deserve for your available truck.

NOTES -

STRATEGY 10 – FIND ONE THING OR A LOT OF THINGS THAT ARE NEGATIVE ABOUT THE LOAD, NOT THE BROKER/3PL

Remember, it's very important to remain calm, likable, polite and sincere, and C.L.A.S.S. You want to gain empathy here. Most brokers know when a load is a miserable ordeal and recognize the need for additional compensation. When they go to their boss for approval for paying you such a high rate, they will take your reasons with them. If you can explain it to them in a way they didn't realize before, it is easier for them to go and get more money approved for this particular load from their customer or boss.

Remember C.L.A.S.S.

Does it tie up your truck for too many hours? Days?

NOTES -

Does it load on a Thursday and deliver on a Monday?

Weight – Too heavy

Shipper – history of delays

Consignee – history of delays

Deadhead Origin - a long way to pick up

Deadhead Destination – it delivers a long way from where you have to pick up your next load

Tolls

Late pick up appointment – losing time, maybe a day

Delivery Time – Late Delivery appointment, you may lose a day

NOTES -

Delivery city – cheap backhauls, last time you went to this particular city, you sat there for two days and then got a cheap backhaul. You don't want to go there in the first place; they called you, but you will slowly, grudgingly entertain the idea.

All of these individual items make good "back burner" items. One or more to be pulled out later when you're closer to settlement, to get that last bit of money left on the table...

NOTES -

STRATEGY 11 – SAY POSITIVE THINGS ABOUT YOUR COMPANY, THE BROKER, YOUR DRIVER

Flattery won't get you everywhere, but it will get you more money on this load. These are comments you want to slip in subtly while negotiating. If the Broker/3PL mentions they have had service issues with this customer and they are worried about it, this is the time for reassurance! Discuss your on- time service approach to all loads. These aren't major negotiating points, but they help build the good will we need to get a premium price on this load. As the conversation goes on, just casually mention that your driver has been with you a long time, he's never late, he's good with customers, etc. Mention how you like doing business with this particular Broker/3PL, and your companies have been doing business a long time. This creates comfort and good will!

NOTES -

STRATEGY 12 – HIGH FUEL COST IS YOUR FRIEND

Brokers/3PL's have held onto fuel surcharges for years and not passed them along proportionally to carriers.

Do not make a general statement or complaint about the price of diesel. Do not go on about how hard it is to make a living now, be specific, and use a real example. "I hauled a similar load a month ago that paid more per mile, and fuel has gone up 5% in the last month.

The higher rate you get shouldn't be directly proportionate to what your actual higher cost of fuel is on the load, in fact, it should be much higher. You have had to cash flow this meteoric rise in fuel the past few years. It would take a rocket scientist or two to figure out how much the rise in fuel prices have

NOTES –

actually cost you. You are just "framing" and letting him know the price will be higher based on that fact alone, not including all of the other strategies/facts you have already brought up. If the Broker/3PL wants to get scientific and explain that it only will cost you "x" more at 6 MPG, etc. Go into detail about the higher fuel costs in states you have to go through and the load weighs 44,000lbs so your fuel will drop to 4 MPG between the weight and the hills...

Remain calm, likeable, specific and unemotional, in your conversation.

Remember C.L.A.S.S. in all your conversations.

Explain your reasons calmly, especially if he or she gets insulted. Try and calm them down, i.e. "I am not trying to be greedy or unrealistic; this is just the reality of hauling

NOTES -

this load. If they won't or can't see the reality, simply thank them for calling and offering the load to you, but maybe it's just not the right fit right now.

NOTES -

STRATEGY 13 – A LOAD OF WHAT? AND WHY DO YOU CARE?

Why do you care? Besides the obvious reasons, HAZMAT, or something that could damage your trailer like trash from the East Coast or used batteries. A very important indicator of how much money the Broker/3PL has in the load is the value of the product. The higher the value, the less concerned the shipper is about price than service. Think of electronics vs. cat litter or mulch. This is just a basic fact of the business. In some cases with mulch or cat litter, the price of the freight exceeds the value of the whole load. This is a simple and quick way to get an idea of what type of negotiating room there is on a specific load.

NOTES -

STRATEGY 14 – LOCATION! LOCATION! LOCATION!

Grocery Warehouse or Major Retailer DC, always get a premium rate and explain why!

It's not just the unloading time, of course you always want to make sure you have detention time agreed to before every load, but it is the "what ifs" that will get you the price here. Think of it as extra money for the risk involved in taking the load, the extra money you will need as insurance against the following:

What happens if you are late? Before you proceed, make sure that the Broker/3PL understands that the only possible reason you are ever late is because of events that are out of your control!

NOTES -

What if your truck is delayed being loaded which causes a late delivery? What if there is a maintenance issue? Traffic or weather? A normal delivery wouldn't be a major ordeal if you were an hour or two late because of legitimate issues. But a major retailer's DC? A grocery warehouse? You will lose a day or two until they can make another appointment for you. You have to build this risk into the cost of the load!! The Broker/3PL knows how bad these receivers are. Bring it up often and tell stories about your bad experiences at these places to help frame the need of your premium rate.

NOTES -

STARTEGY 15 – THANK AND COMPLIMENT THE BROKER FOR HIS BUSINESS, HIS TIME, OR BOTH! EVERY TIME!!

This is imperative. You want the Broker/3PL to be as satisfied and confident in his decision on this transaction as you are! You want to do a good job and get more business in the future. Give the Broker/3PL their money's worth.

Your professionalism and your gratitude will be long remembered and rewarded.

NOTES -

Visit www.18wheelsofjustice.com for information on future publications, contact information and additional merchandise.

Also available by special order in Spanish, Russian, Polish, Turkish and Indian translations.

13420696R00065

Made in the USA
Charleston, SC
09 July 2012